February 1982

DIESELS
and
ELECTRICS
ON SHED
(Volume Three)
WESTERN REGION

DIESELS and ELECTRICS ON SHED

(Volume Three)
WESTERN REGION
by Rex Kennedy

Oxford Publishing Co. Oxford

Oxford Publishing Co. 1981

ISBN 0 86093 042 4

ACKNOWLEDGEMENTS
My thanks, once again, go to the many railway photo-
graphers who have contributed to this album, and also to
the enthusiasts who have helped me trace pictures of
locations rarely photographed. Many thanks also, go to my
wife, Pauline, who has spent countless hours typing
captions and information for this volume.

Half Title Page
No. D1070 *Western Gauntlet* protrudes from the entrance
of the refuelling depot at Cardiff Canton.

John Vaughan

Frontispiece
Resting over the pits at Old Oak Common, HST set No.
253 031 displays its tow-bar mechanism on 7th October
1979.

David Maxey

Title Page
Main line motive power stands in the fuelling depot at
Cardiff Canton. Preparing to resume duties No. 47 105
stands alongside No. 45 043 *The King's Own Royal
Border Regiment* on 6th January 1978.

Michael Rhodes

Printed by:
Blackwell's in the City of Oxford

Published by:
Oxford Publishing Co.,
8 The Roundway,
Headington,
Oxford.

Beyer-Peacock Class 35 'Hymek' locomotive No. D7077 ▶
stands in the yard adjoining Barry Depot in August 1971.

Norman Kneale

INTRODUCTION

Many changes have been seen on the Western Region of British Rail in the form of motive power since the introduction of diesel traction, and I have tried to portray as many of these as possible in this third volume of *Diesels and Electrics on Shed.*

Views of electric locomotives on this region are, of course, rare, except where they are in the course of transportation to the scrapyard or at an 'Open Day', although Southern Region electro-diesels have been seen at Reading, Swindon and Oxford depots in service.

The 'Warship' and 'Western', once the pride of the West Country routes, replacing the Great Western 'Castles' and 'Kings' have now, alas, gone, firstly to be replaced by the introduction of more Class 46 'Peaks' to the region and then with the entire complement of Class 50 locomotives arriving from the London Midland Region. The HSTs now run to Penzance in the West Country, deep into South Wales, and at Paddington, High Speed Trains now outnumber locomotive hauled expresses.

The D95XX Paxman Hydraulic, introduced in 1964 for short-haul freight work, disappeared with the abandonment of Diesel Hydraulic traction after most of the class made the long journey to Hull Dairycoates Depot for a short-lived stay.

Depots in the Birmingham area once under the control of Western Region became London Midland Region controlled, and at first it was difficult to fix in the mind of the older railway enthusiast that sheds like Tyseley and Stourbridge Junction were no longer Western Region depots. Certain depots which once serviced and maintained vast quantities of steam locomotives now are just mere stabling or fuelling points, like Oxford, Taunton or Aberdare.

Even Ranelagh Bridge Yard, the point where all locospotters look when leaving Paddington by train with the hope of seeing something new, is often bare since the introduction of the HST.

New purpose-built depot buildings are now springing up, like the HST depot at Penzance and the two small single-road buildings at Exeter St. David's and Carmarthen, but a few of the old Great Western brick structures remain.

St. Blazey, in particular, with its half roundhouse and outside turntable, still portrays that wonderful atmosphere of history, nostalgia and the railways. One can stand there and picture a whole lifetime of railway activity from Great Western 'Halls' to 'Western' Hydraulics and now 47s and 37s.

When we hear the words 'Western Region', we automatically still think 'Western' and 'Warship', but we must all move with the times.

The interest in railways and particularly the activities around the depots will always be there for the enthusiast, and I hope this book will please both the new modern enthusiast and the enthusiast who remembers the green and maroon liveries of the Western Region diesels.

Rex Kennedy
Oxford 1981

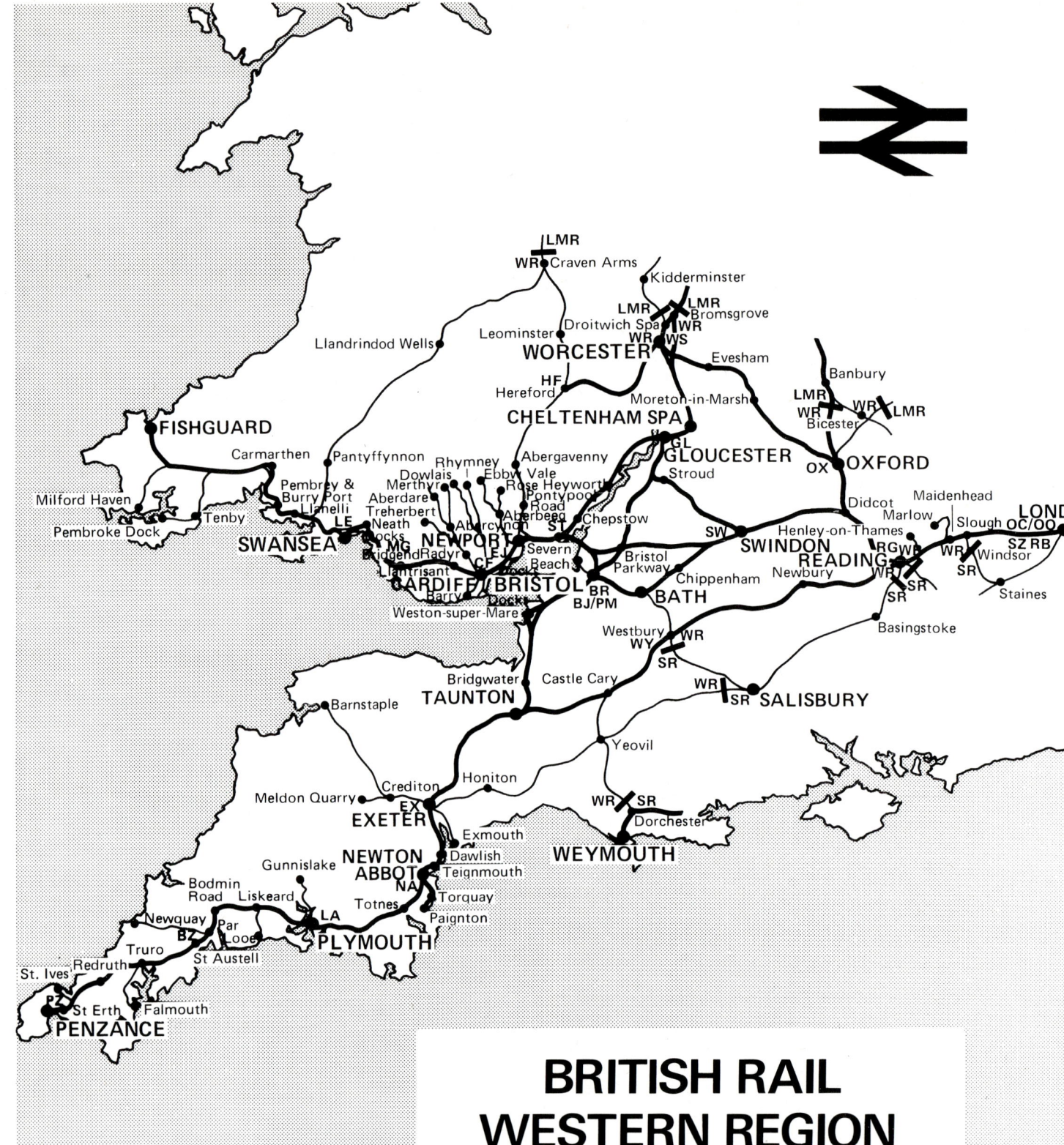

BRITISH RAIL
WESTERN REGION

showing regional boundaries, depots and fuelling points

BRITISH RAILWAYS MOTIVE POWER DEPOTS, FUELLING POINTS and STABLING POINTS
of the WESTERN REGION portrayed in this volume

	Location	Code	Old Code	Plate
LONDON DIVISION	Old Oak Common Maintenance & HST Depots	OC/OO	81A	1 — 27
	Ranelagh Bridge Fuelling Point	RB	—	28 — 29
	Southall D.M.U. Depot	SZ	81C	30 — 31
	Reading Maintenance Depot	RG	81D	32 — 37
	Oxford Servicing Depot	OX	81F	38 — 42
BRISTOL DIVISION	Bristol (Bath Road) Maintenance Depot	BR	82A	43 — 60
	Bristol Marsh Junction D.M.U. Depot	BJ	—	61 — 62
	St. Philip's Marsh HST Depot	PM	—	63 — 65
	Swindon Servicing Depot	SW	82C	66 — 69
	Westbury Servicing Depot	WY	82D/83C	70 — 73
	Bath (Green Park) Depot	—	82F	74
	Newton Abbot Servicing Depot	NA	83A	75 — 85
	Exeter (St. David's) Fuelling Point	EX	83C	86 — 88
	Taunton Stabling Point	—	83B	89
	Plymouth (Laira) Maintenance Depot	LA	83D/84A	90 — 104
	St. Blazey Servicing Depot	BZ	83E/84B	105 — 111
	Meldon Quarry Stabling Point	—	—	112
	Penzance Servicing Depot & Stabling Point	PZ	83G/84D	113 — 116
	Worcester Servicing Depot	WS	85A	117 — 120
	Gloucester Servicing Depot	GL	85B	121 — 128
	Bromsgrove Stabling Point	—	85D	129
CARDIFF DIVISION	Hereford Fuelling Point	HF	85C	130
	Newport (Ebbw Junction) Maintenance Depot	EJ	86A/86B	131 — 140
	Newport Docks Stabling Point	—	86B	141
	Aberbeeg Stabling Point	—	86H	142 — 143
	Pontypool Road Depot	—	86G	144
	Severn Tunnel Junction Servicing Depot	ST	86E	145 — 150
	Cardiff (Canton) Maintenance Depot	CF	86C/86A	151 — 176
	Cardiff Docks Stabling Points	—	88B (Sub)	177 — 178
	Radyr Depot & Stabling Point	—	88A (Sub)	179 — 181
	Barry Depot	—	88C	182 — 183
	Llantrisant Depot & Stabling Point	—	86D	184 — 185
	Rhymney Stabling Point	—	88D (Sub)	186 — 187
	Dowlais (Cae Harris) Depot	—	88D (Sub)	188
	Treherbert Depot	—	88F	189
	Abercynon Depot	—	88E	190
	Aberdare Depot & Stabling Point	—	86J	191 — 192
	Margam Maintenance Depot	MG	87B	193 — 200
	Landore (Swansea) Maintenance Depot	LE	87E/87A	201 — 206
	Swansea East Dock Stabling Point	—	87D	207
	Neath (N&B) Depot	—	87A (Sub)	208
	Llanelli Stabling Point	—	87F	209 — 210
	Burry Port Stabling Point	—	87F (Sub)	211
	Carmarthen Stabling Point	—	87G	212
	Pantyffynnon Stabling Point	—	87F (Sub)	213

OLD OAK COMMON

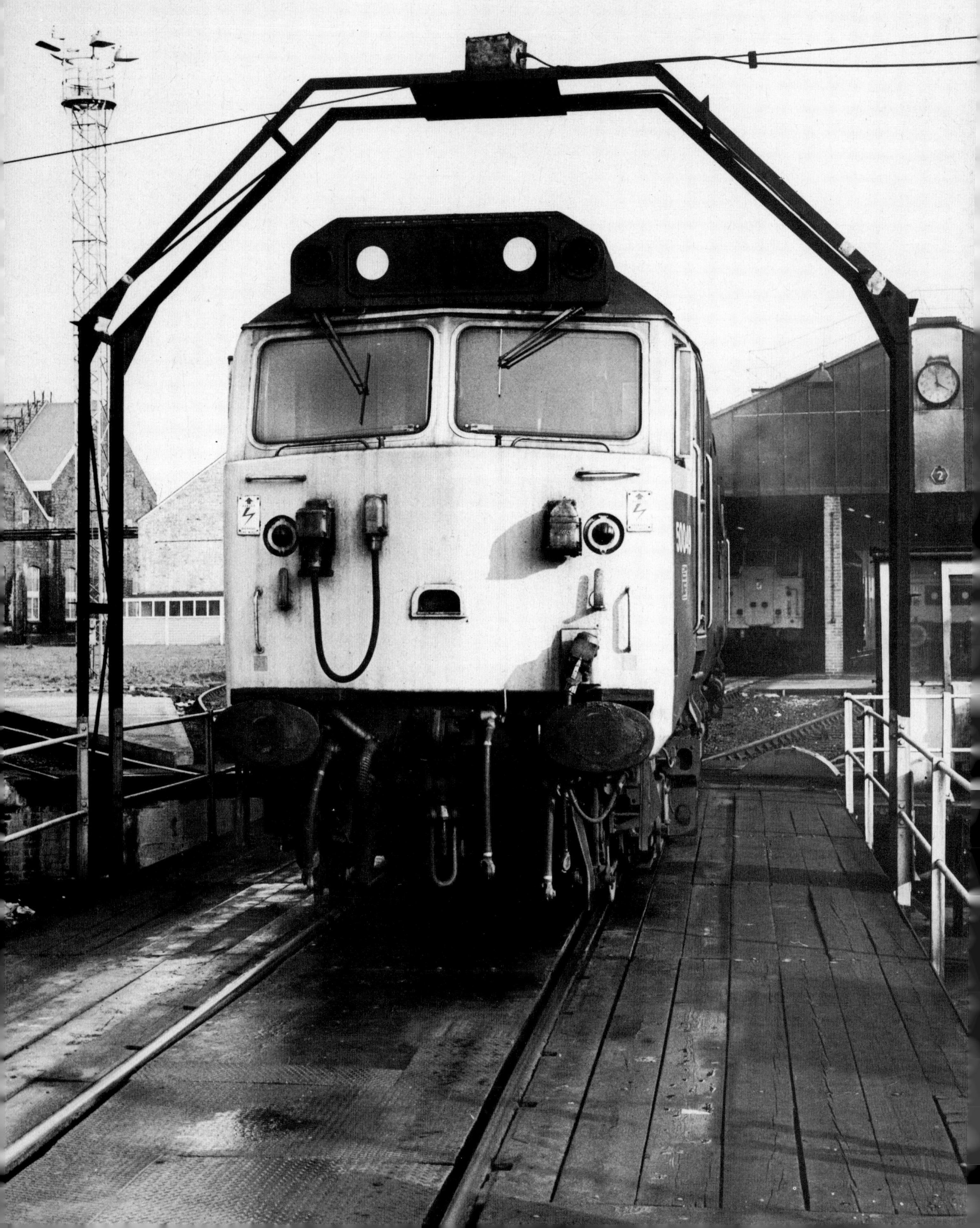

1 Class 50 No. 50 049 *Defiance* slowly moves on to the turntable at Old Oak Common Depot on 28th February 1980.
Colin Marsden

2 Class 47s and 31s encircle the turntable at Old Oak Common on 28th February 1980. With the fuelling depot seen in the background, Class 47 No. 47 029 makes full use of the short stretch of track allocated for each locomotive which helps to form the 'spider's web' effect on the railway turntable system.

Colin Marsden

Turntable Scenes

3 The crew of Class 52 'Western' No. D1013 *Western Ranger* prepare to rotate the locomotive on the turntable on 21st July 1975.
Graham Scott-Lowe

Class 252, 253 and 254

4 A Class 08 shunter moves HST prototype power car No. 252 001 at Old Oak Common on 17th August 1975. This power car was introduced on to British Railways in 1972 and was originally numbered 41 001.

Graham Scott-Lowe

5 Beneath the vast roof of Old Oak Common carriage shed, HST set No. 253 028 waits in a comparatively empty depot before returning to duty on 7th October 1979.

David Maxey

6 A stranger in the camp. The unusual sight of a 254 Class HST now operating on the Eastern Region, standing in the HST depot at Old Oak Common on 2nd April 1978. At this time, a number of Class 254 sets were on loan to the Western Region before their introduction on the East Coast Main Line.

David Maxey

7   Looking out from the darkness of the fuelling depot at Old Oak Common is seen Class 52 'Western' No. 1052 *Western Viceroy* with Class 47 No. 47 089 *Amazon* standing beyond the turntable on 17th August 1975.   *Graham Scott-Lowe*

8   Almost forming a 'guard of honour' for Class 52 'Western' No. D1048 *Western Lady* are the standard lamps in the turntable yard at Old Oak Common.

John Vaughan

The 'Western'

9 Two gas turbine locomotives Nos. 18000 and 18100 were introduced onto British Railways in 1950 and 1952 respectively. Both these locomotives were allocated to Old Oak Common and No. 18000 is pictured here on that depot. This locomotive was built by the Swiss firm Brown-Boveri and used a gas turbine engine to drive an electric generator which provided power for the electric motors. No. 18100 was later converted by Metro-Vickers to become an electric locomotive No. E2001, formerly E1000.

John Oatway

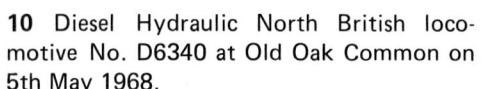

10 Diesel Hydraulic North British locomotive No. D6340 at Old Oak Common on 5th May 1968.

David Wood

11 Class 31 Brush Type 2 locomotive No. 5539 was one of the Class 31s to be transferred from the Eastern to the Western Region. It is seen here on 21st April 1971 at Old Oak Common.

Peter Groon

Hydraulics

12 Standing proudly outside the repair shops at Old Oak Common and sporting its fine roundel BR crest is Class 52 'Western' Diesel Hydraulic No. D1004 *Western Crusader* on 17th August 1962.

Peter Groom

13 Unfortunately the days have now gone when BR diesels and electrics displayed their route destination headcodes. On this occasion on 13th April 1962 can be seen at Old Oak Common two 'Warship' Class diesels, with No. D817 *Foxhound* nearest the camera.

Peter Groom

14 Beyer-Peacock Class 35 'Hymek' No. D7049 waits outside the depot at Old Oak Common on 29th October 1962. This class of hydraulic locomotive was introduced onto British Railways in 1961, the first one in the Class No. D7000 being handed over at a short ceremony in Paddington station on 16th May 1961.

Peter Groom

17 With newly painted pipes and in immaculate condition in preparation for an enthusiasts' special, No. 47 508 stands in the repair shop at Old Oak Common. When this photograph was taken on 2nd April 1978 the locomotive was allocated to Landore and a year later was transferred to Old Oak Common and named *Great Britain*.

David Maxey

18 Surrounded by the environment of the repair shop at Old Oak Common two Class 31 locomotives, one with converted headboard panel, await maintenance on 2nd April 1978. The locomotives on view are Nos. 31 286 and 31 260.

David Maxey

Undergoing Maintenance

15 Undergoing major maintenance at Old Oak Common on 20th October 1978, Class 47 No. 47 500 is held aloft and appears to be minus one windscreen.

Colin Marsden

16 HST power car No. W43004 of set 253 002 undergoes repair on 12th May 1980 in the Old Oak Common factory which is another name for the repair shop.

Colin Marsden

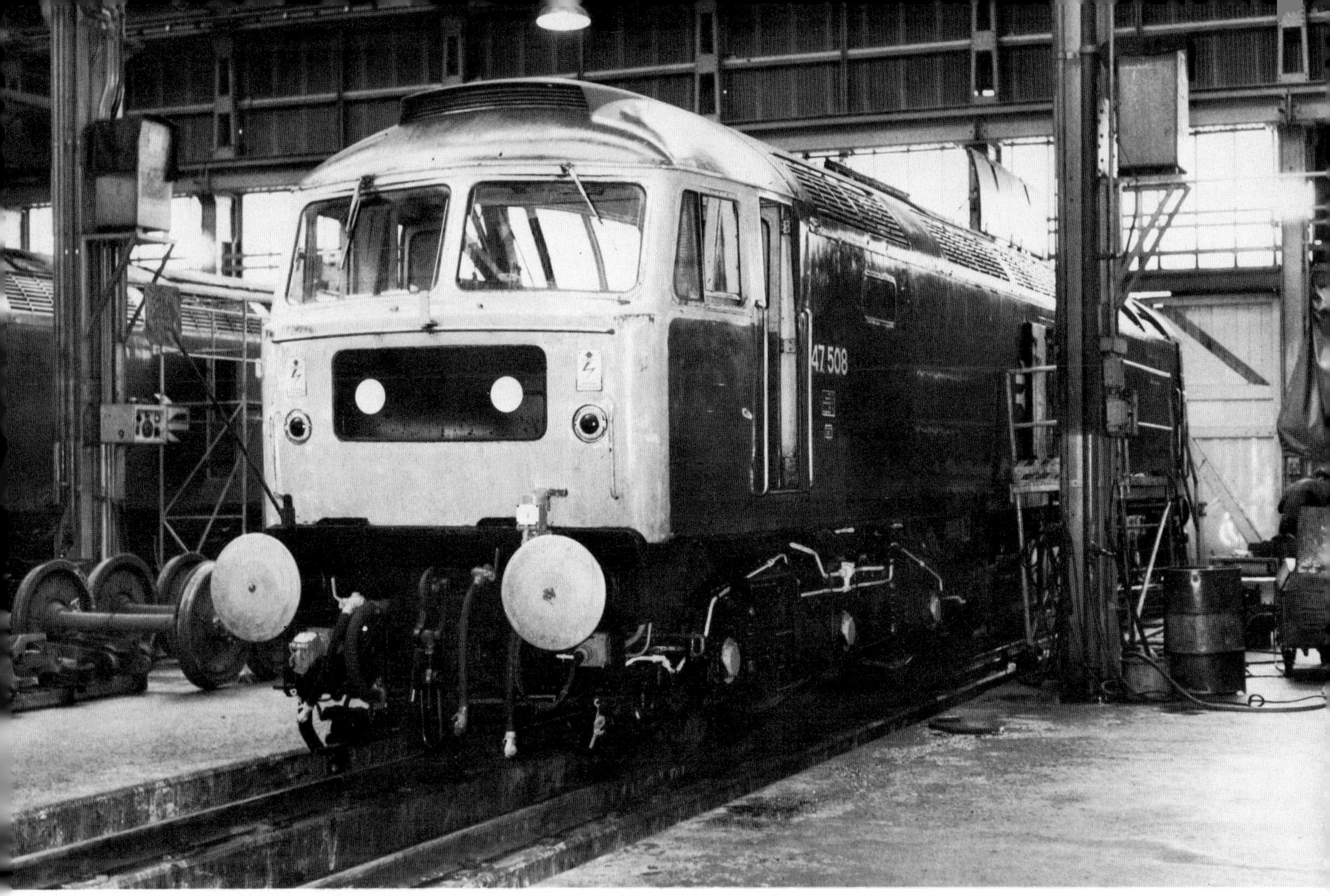
47 508

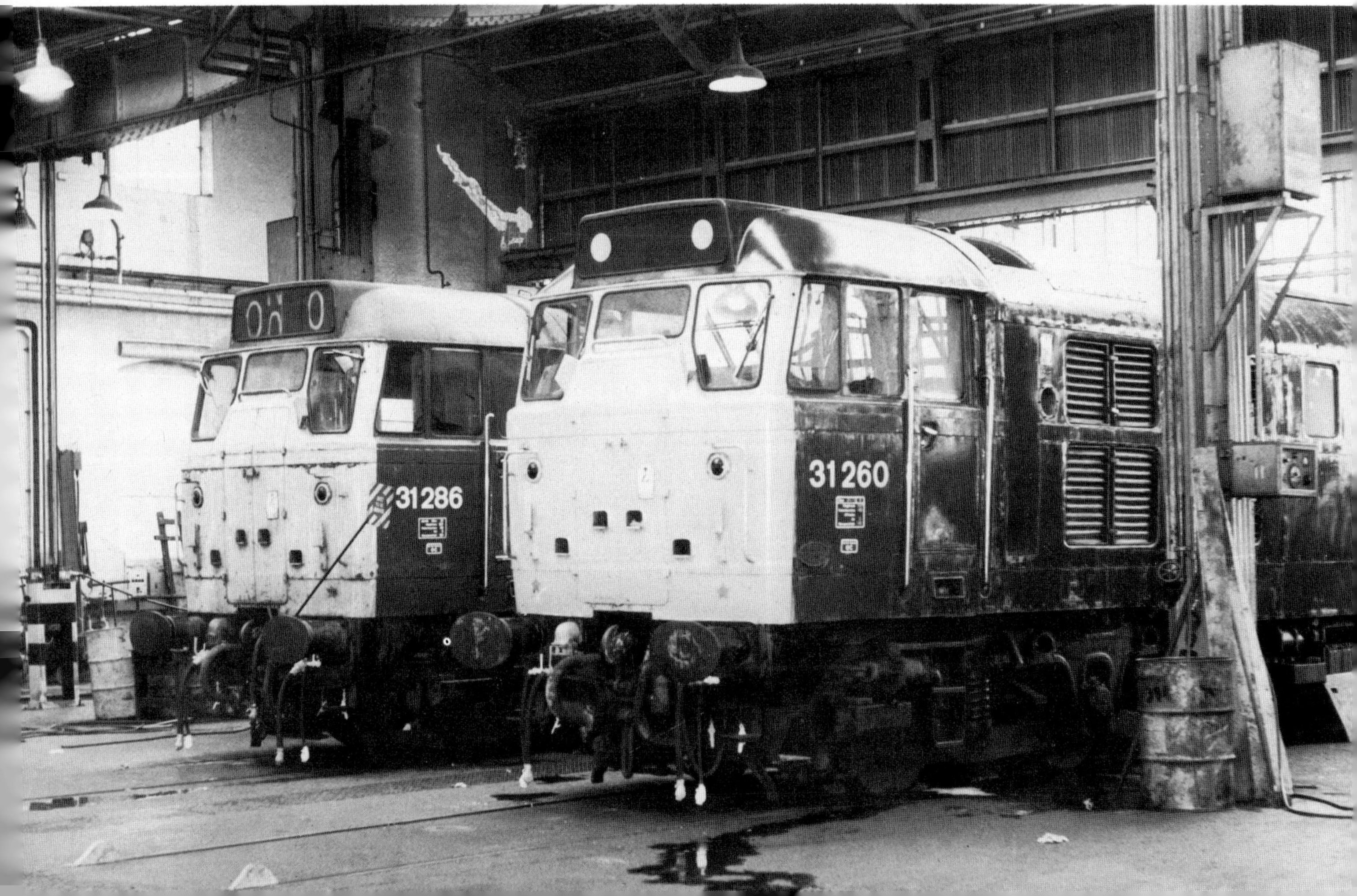
31286
31260

Fuelling Point

19 A trio of Class 47 diesels guard the turntable end of the fuelling and servicing depot at Old Oak Common on 28th February 1980. From left to right are Nos. 47 484 with e.t.h. and modified front end panel, 47 028 fitted for steam heating with standard front end panel and 47 507 with e.t.h. and standard front end panel.

Colin Marsden

20 Class 50s at Old Oak Common on 17th October 1978. No. 50 010 *Monarch* waits outside the fuelling depot whilst inside, are seen Nos. 50 001 *Dreadnought* and 50 025 *Invincible* preparing for their next turn of duty. The entire class of this locomotive was transferred from the London Midland Region to the Western Region with the demise of the Class 52 'Westerns'.

Colin Marsden

21 Basking in the sunlight with the repair shops at Old Oak Common in the background are two Class 47 locomotives with No. 47 485 in the foreground.

Colin Marsden

22 A line of three Class 50s stand off duty in Old Oak Common yard on 5th November 1978. The locomotives pictured are Nos. 50 036 *Victorious*, 50 041 *Bulwark* and 50 032 *Courageous*.

Graham Scott-Lowe

23 Pictured after a storm at Old Oak Common, Class 08 shunter No. 08 798 is mirrored in the pool which has formed between the track outside the repair shop on 20th January 1980.

Rex Kennedy

Unusual Visitors

24 An unusual visitor to Old Oak Common is the Class 56 locomotive. On 26th July 1980, No. 56 045 appeared on shed, probably having worked the Danygraig to Acton freightliner train.

John Vaughan

25 Class 55 'Deltics' are usually only seen at Old Oak Common when used on enthusiasts' specials. The rare sight of No. 55 003 *Meld* as she leaves the depot on 5th March 1978 to haul a special from Paddington is pictured here. This locomotive had to spend the night at Old Oak Common due to the closure of the North London line for track working.

John Vaughan

26 Electric locomotives are rarely found on Western Region depots and often only on Open Days or in transit to the scrap yard. On this occasion three Class 71 electric locomotives Nos. 71 005, 71 006 and 71 012 stop en route from Ashford to a scrap yard in Swansea on 23rd August 1978 after being in service approximately 20 years.

Graham Scott-Lowe

Electrics

27 A mixture of traction was gathered together for the BR Open Day at Old Oak Common on 22nd February 1975. The prototype HST No. 252 001 sits behind Class 86 electric locomotive No. 86 249, in company with two Class 52 'Westerns' Nos. 1022 *Western Sentinel* and 1058 *Western Nobleman*. The Class 08 shunter in attendance is No. 08 678.

Alan Wilson

RANELAGH BRIDGE YARD

28 Ranelagh Bridge Yard situated near Royal Oak station just outside Paddington, has always been the stabling point for main line locomotives waiting to take out trains from Paddington station. As in the steam days locomotives are still dwarfed by the tenement buildings which overlook this site, and on this occasion, on 25th April 1973, Class 52 'Western' No. 1071 *Western Renown* stands against the buffers.

Brian Morrison

29 Locomotives await refuelling at Ranelagh Bridge Yard stabling point on 22nd July 1978. Class 47 No. 47 505 stands over the inspection pit next to the fuelling point and is flanked by Class 50 No. 50 012 *Benbow* and Class 47 No. 47 246. This fine view from above shows the intricate track work around the stabling point.

Les Nixon

SOUTHALL

30 Southall D.M.U. depot rarely sees main line diesels and apart from the units only three or four shunters operate from here. This location is renowned for its single car units, and standing over the inspection pit in the depot on 10th April 1980 is Class 121 Pressed Steel unit No. W55020 next to a Class 117/2 three-car Pressed Steel suburban set, the leading car being No. W51332.

Andrew Kennedy

31 A fine study of an immaculate Class 121 Pressed Steel single-car unit, No. W55021 at Southall on 20th March 1976. The depot building can be seen in the background.

Brian Morrison

READING

32 Reading Depot is situated at the Didcot end of the station, and sees a variety of locomotives including Class 33s from the Southern Region. On this occasion on 7th April 1976 looking out from the depot entrance in the direction of the station we see Class 52 'Western' No. 1028 *Western Hussar* in the distance with Class 31s Nos. 31 421 in the foreground and 31 322 on the right of the picture.

Brian Morrison

33 Class 22 North British Diesel Hydraulic No. D6342 stands outside the depot entrance at Reading on 19th June 1966.

Roger Lamb

34 Sporting the old green livery Class 47 No. D1710 later renumbered 47 121, waits alongside the modern depot building at Reading on 19th June 1966.

Roger Lamb

Shunters at Reading

35 Departmental locomotive No. 20, Ruston and Hornsby 0-4-0 shunter, generally carries out its duties at Reading signal works near to the station. On this occasion it is seen beside the main diesel depot at Reading on 20th June 1971.

Alan Clarke

38 Captured by the sunlight on 5th July 1980, two Class 08 shunters Nos. 08 799 and 08 592 stand with track maintenance equipment at Oxford stabling point. Oxford-based shunters are now officially allocated to Reading Depot.

Rex Kennedy

36 The permanent way shunter No. PWM 653 which is often to be found in the yard at Theale frequently returns to the main depot at Reading. This locomotive, one of five in the class built by Ruston and Hornsby, was introduced in 1953 and is pictured here, at Reading, on 21st August 1972.

Peter Groom

37 Standing outside the closed doors of Reading Depot on 8th November 1975, is Class 08 shunter 08 791, previously numbered D3959.

David Habgood

39 Oxford, once the site of a major steam depot, is now reduced to a small fuelling point and a few shunters which work on nearby duties. On 16th October 1976 a named Class 47, No. 47 079 *George Jackson Churchward*, stands over the pit at this location.

Brian Morrison

40 On rare occasions a Class 56 locomotive is to be found on the stabling point at Oxford. These locomotives regularly pass through Oxford with merry-go-round trains from the North heading for Didcot Power Station. On 29th September 1978 No. 56 044 was seen stabled here beside Class 31 No. 31326.

John Augustson

41 Under the watchful eye of the church, Class 31 No. 31 118 and an 08 shunter stand amongst miscellanea around the depot yard at Oxford.

Andrew Kennedy

43 At the end of steam, when diesel hydraulic took the Western Region by storm, a new diesel depot needed to be constructed at Bristol Bath Road. The construction work at this depot is shown in this picture. Locomotives on view include 'Warships', 'Peaks' and 'Hymeks'.

British Rail

44 The completed diesel depot at Bristol Bath Road as it stands today. The addition of the yard lamps is apparent, conveying improvements made over the years. A variety of classes are represented in this view taken on 21st June 1980, including 'Peaks', Class 31s, Class 50s, Class 47s, D.M.Us and Class 25s.

Rex Kennedy

42 A view from the station end of the fuelling and stabling point at Oxford sees Class 47 No. 47 329 and Class 31 No. 31 123 on March 22nd 1980. The carriage sidings and lines to Worcester and Birmingham are seen in the distance.

Andrew Kennedy

BRISTOL (Bath Road)

Turntable Scenes

45 This view of Class 47 No. 47 142 at Bristol Bath Road on 21st October 1979 is photographed from an unusual angle and shows the full extent of the turntable and its operation.

David Maxey

46 Bristol Bath Road Depot turntable is situated at the rear of the depot. Class 45 'Peak' locomotive No. 45 011 provides a perfect fit on the turntable, before moving off to another part of the depot on 1st October 1978.

David Maxey

47 An unusual visitor to Bristol Bath Road is Class 84 Electric Locomotive No. E3044, later numbered 84 009. This locomotive had been brought to Bristol on this occasion for an Open Day and the smoke from a steam engine also imported for the occasion can be seen drifting above.

South Devon Railway Museum

48 Southern Region allocated Class 33s quite regularly work to Bristol and on 21st June 1980 No. 33 025 from Eastleigh rests on the turntable.

Graham Scott-Lowe

49 Class 40 locomotives are one of the rarer visitors to Bristol Bath Road Depot, but on this occasion on 7th June 1980 No. 40 155 was to be found standing alongside the depot.

Graham Scott-Lowe

50 Class 50 No. 50 017 *Royal Oak* prepares to move off the depot at Bristol Bath Road on 8th March 1980. It is noticeable that this locomotive is fitted with a blanking plate where the headlight normally appears. No. 50 017 was the second Class 50 to be refurbished at Doncaster Works after No. 50 006 *Neptune*, and at this time the headlights were not available. However, all electrical work was carried out for the eventual headlight fitting which took place in February 1981 at Plymouth (Laira).
John Hillmer

51 Class 47 No. 47 189 takes a wash as it eases its way through the washing plant at Bristol Bath Road Depot on 23rd August 1980.

John Chalcraft

52 The powerful designs of the English Electric and Sulzer main line diesels are portrayed in this picture at Bristol Bath Road. Outside the maintenance depot stand Class 40 No. 40 044 beside Class 45 'Peak' No. 45 052 and an unidentified Class 46 locomotive on 21st June 1980.

Graham Scott-Lowe

Class 47s at Bath Road

33 It is appropriate that many of the names given to the diesels which now run on the Western Region are the ones once carried by Great Western locomotives that travelled the same routes. Class 47 No. 47 077 *North Star* is one of these locomotives and is pictured here on 21st June 1980 in the yard at Bristol Bath Road.

Rex Kennedy

34 In the days when the enthusiast still had the opportunity of seeing headcodes correctly displayed in their panels, Class 47 No. 47 035 waits off duty outside the fuelling depot at Bristol Bath Road on 4th May 1975.

Graham Scott-Lowe

Hydraulics

55 Two Class 52 'Western' locomotives Nos. 1010 *Western Campaigner* and 1048 *Western Lady* wait at Bristol Bath Road Depot en route to Newton Abbot on their last day in service on 26th February 1977.

Graham Scott-Lowe

56 Class 22 North British Hydraulics stand in line at Bristol Bath Road on 28th March 1971. No. 6308 leads Nos. D6328 and D6320. It is noticeable that since the deletion of the letter 'D' from the number of the leading locomotive, the British Rail symbol appears above the number and not below.

Alan Clarke

57 Class 37 locomotives are never found in abundance at Bristol Bath Road Depot, but on this occasion on 2nd April 1978 Nos. 37 296 and 37 298 stand together over the inspection pits.

Graham Scott-Lowe

58 The refuelling shed at Bristol Bath Road is a three-road building and a variety of main line traction passes through constantly during the day. On 1st October 1978 Class 50 No. 50 014 *Warspite* stands alongside Class 47 No. 47 468.

David Maxey

Bath Road at Night

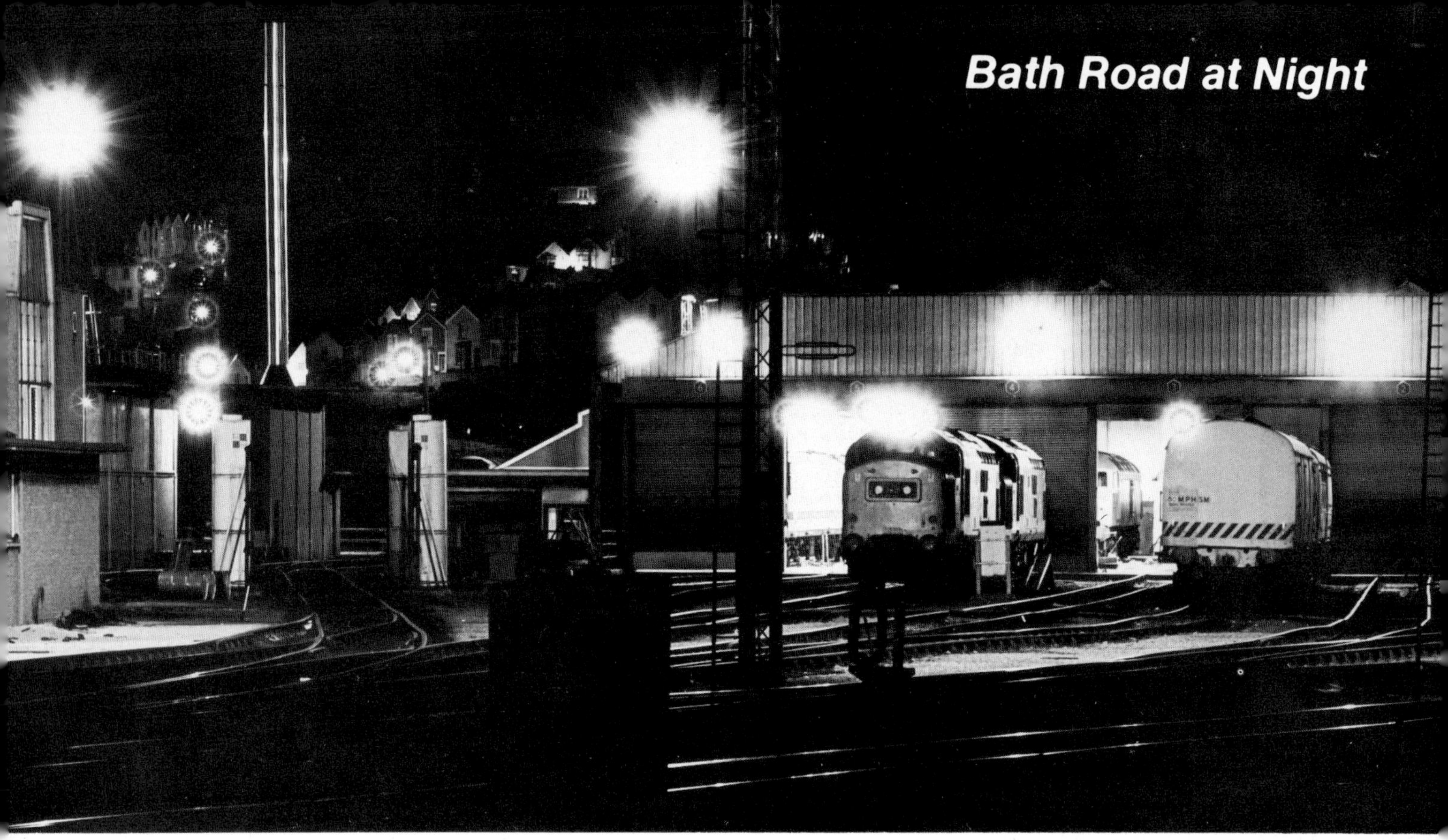

59 The late evening on any depot creates a fascinating scene. This view of Bristol Bath Road actually taken in the early hours of the morning of 15th September 1979 shows two Class 37s standing outside the depot with a starlight effect being created by the yard lights.

John Hillmer

60 Locomotive crews often have to report for duty in the very early hours of the morning, and on 22nd May 1976 Class 52 'Western' No. D1013 *Western Ranger* moves off the turn-table in readiness to work the 6000 Locomotive Association's 'Merchant Venturer' rail tour later in the day.

Graham Scott-Lowe

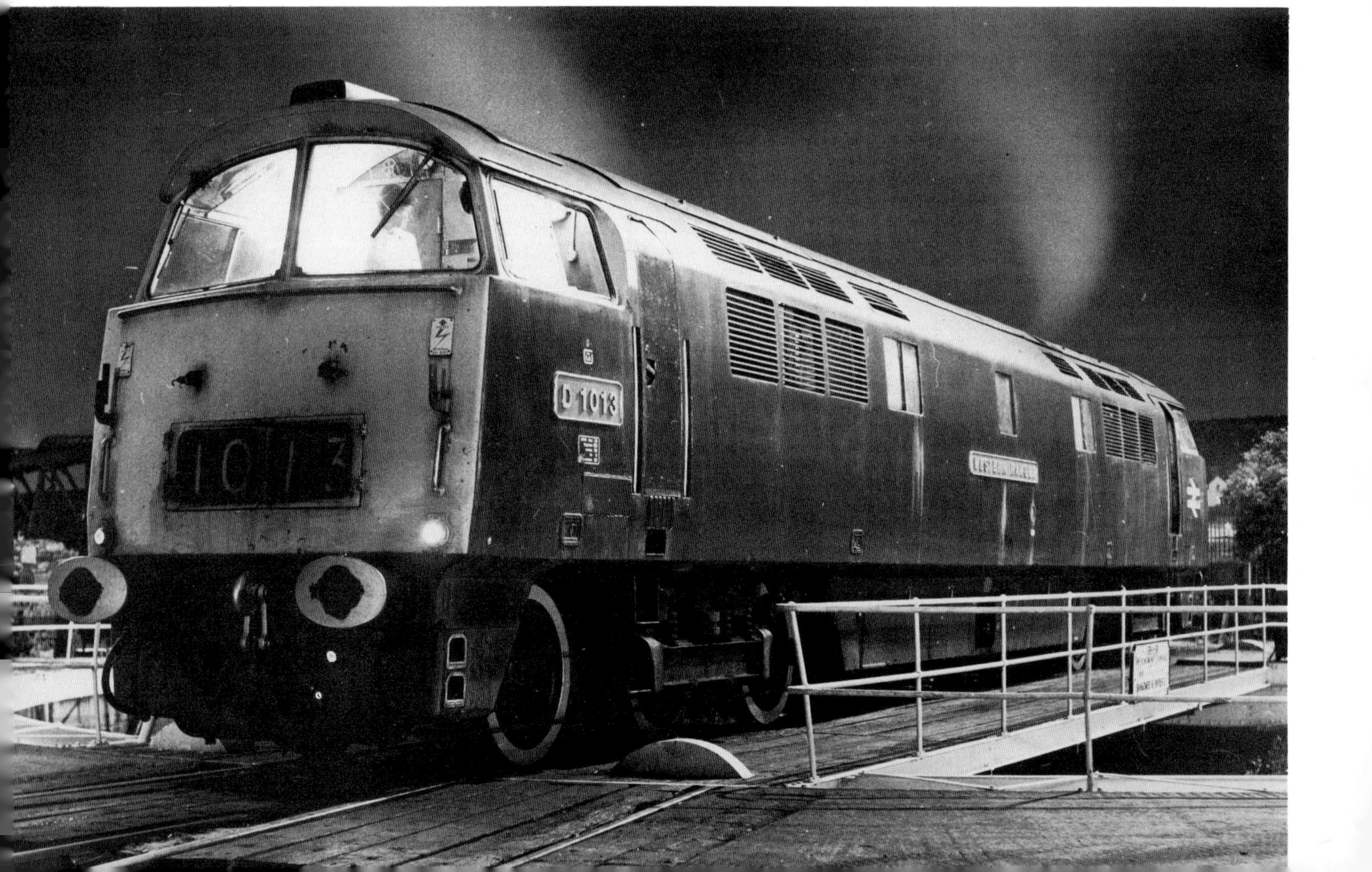

MARSH JUNCTION
(D.M.U.) Depot

61 The fuelling point at Marsh Junction, Bristol is situated half way between the maintenance depot for D.M.Us and the old St. Philip's Marsh steam shed which was a huge roundhouse. Looking towards the old steam shed a Gloucester three-car cross-country set stands at the fuelling point on 2nd February 1959, with signs of steam in the background.

British Rail

62 Soon after the building of the D.M.U. depot at Marsh Junction, Bristol, Gloucester three-car cross-country sets took up residence in this building. In this picture both the building, its interior and the trains too, are in immaculate condition.

British Rail

63 With the introduction of the High Speed Trains onto the Western Region, St. Philip's Marsh, Bristol was a location chosen for a maintenance depot. Power cars Nos. W43007 and W43010 bask in the sunlight outside the depot building on 23rd August 1976.

Barry Nicolle

ST. PHILIP'S MARSH H.S.T. DEPOT

64 The power car from HST set No. 253 003 receives maintenance in an otherwise empty depot at St. Philip's Marsh, Bristol, on 17th August 1976.

Graham Scott-Lowe

65 Whilst out of service, Western Region HST sets stand in the yard at St. Philip's Marsh HST depot. The trio pictured here on 18th September 1976 are Nos. 253 003, 253 005 and 253 007.

Graham Scott-Lowe

SWINDON

66 The old steam depot at Swindon also saw a good selection of diesels at that site prior to the building going out of use. On 22nd March 1964 Class 40 No. D377, later to be renumbered 40 177, stands with a 'Hymek' outside the shed alongside an ex-Great Western steam locomotive.

Colin Caddy

67 Two North British Class 22 Diesel Hydraulics Nos. D6331 and D6321 are pictured over the pits outside Swindon shed early in 1964. These are the pits that once frequently saw hot ashes from the boilers of the old Great Western locomotives.

Norman Preedy

68 After the old steam depot was no longer used to house diesel locomotives, a new fuelling point was built between the locomotive works, which can be seen in the background on this picture, and the station. On 25th January 1981, Class 37 No. 37 183 stands near the fuelling point with the line to Stroud and Gloucester going away to the right, in front of the works which were built by the Great Western Railway. Class 37 locomotives refuel at Swindon after being used in the area on various freight workings, predominantly stone trains.

Rex Kennedy

70 Westbury has always been an interesting location both in steam and diesel days, but now only carries facilities for fuelling diesel locomotives. This general view, as seen from the station on 29th March 1975, shows a selection of traction stabled including Class 47s, Class 52 'Westerns' and even a D.M.U. amongst other locomotives.

Bert Wynn

69 A new Class 03 shunter N D2157, pictured here on 2' August 1960, stands immacula in green livery at Swind depot. This locomotive, la renumbered 03 157 and n withdrawn, spent the majori of its life at Hull Botar Gardens.

Alec Swa

71 Three main line diesels pictured at Westbury on the evening of 15th May 1978 are Class 45 'Peak' No. 45 052, Class 33 No. 33 059 and Class 47 No. 47 124.

South Devon Railway Museum

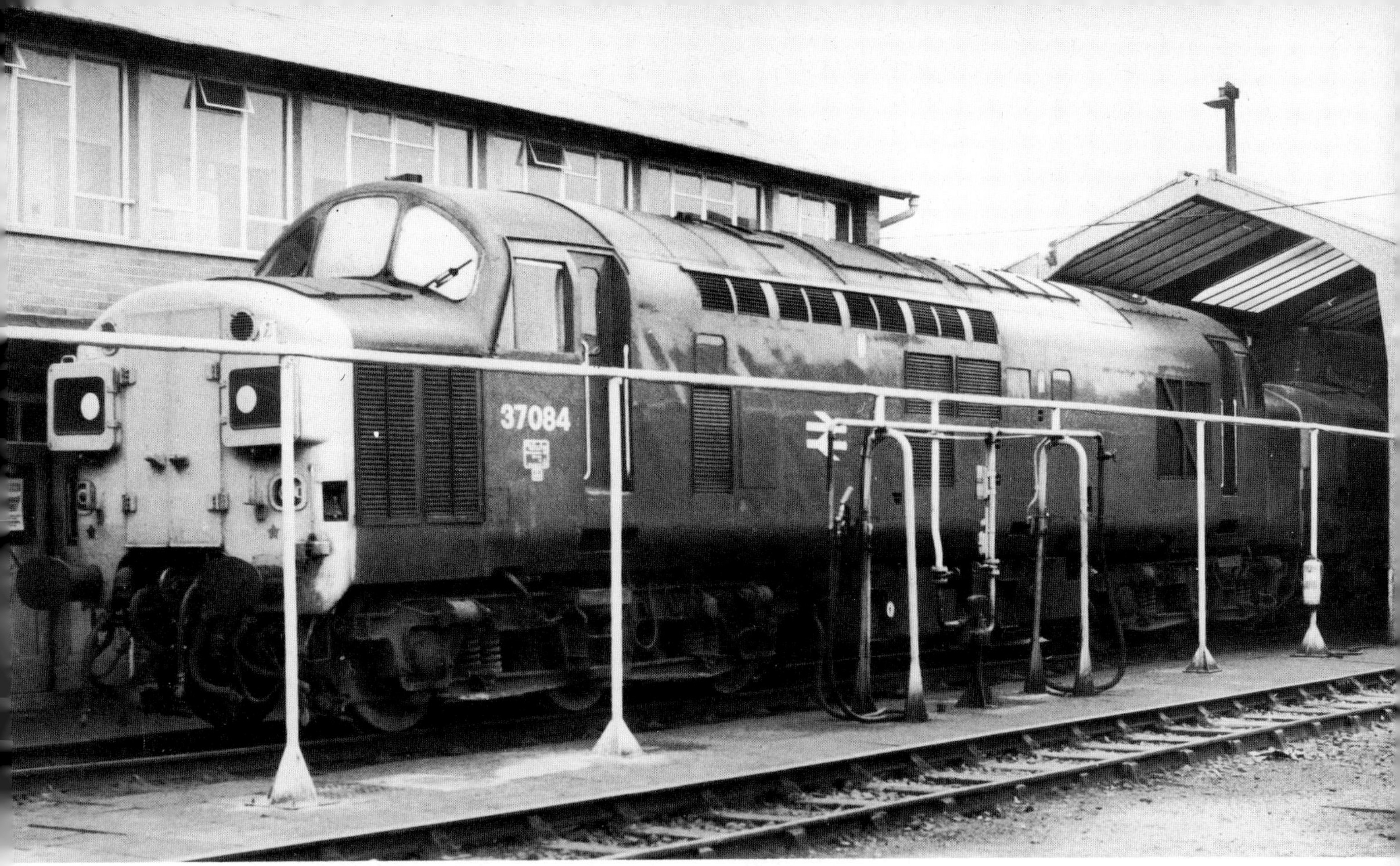

73 Captured in the fuelling bay on 21st April 1979, and overlooked by the office block at Westbury, is Class 37 No. 37 084 allocated to March Depot on the Eastern Region.

Graham Wise

74 A location that no longer sees the stabling of diesel locomotives is Bath (Green Park). 'Peak' No. D116 from the London Midland Region bearing its 16C shed plate beneath the indicator panel, stands beside the old steam depot and carries the old green livery.

Grenville Hounsell

BATH (Green Park)

2 The portal of the fuelling bay at Westbury provides a frame for Class 47 No. 47 243 on 5th July 1980. Locomotives stabled here are more often than not used on stone trains to and from Merehead and Whatley quarries.

John Vaughan

NEWTON ABBOT

75 Newton Abbot has always been a fascinating location and the depot area covers a large expanse. This picture taken on 2nd July 1979 shows the varying levels of track work and provides the opportunity to see two Class 46 'Peaks', one on the lower level at the fuelling point being No. 46 033 and its companion on the higher level No. 46 056.

Brian Morrison

76 The interior of the fuelling shed at Newton Abbot on 2nd July 1979 provides cover for Class 45 'Peak' No. 45 028 prior to refuelling. Class 31 No. 31 273 and a Class 46 locomotive are also pictured.

Brian Morrison

77 This fine side view of Class 52 'Western' No. 1010 *Western Campaigner* also shows the Newton Abbot Depot building in the background on 15th August 1976. The Class 52 'Westerns' were built at Swindon and Crewe and were introduced in 1961 to work on the Great Western routes to the West Country, once operated by 'Castles' and 'Kings'. The lettering on the nameplates was the traditional Great Western lettering used on the nameplates of the steam locomotives.

Peter Gater

78 Southern Region Class 33 diesels occasionally operate west of Exeter and on 16th August 1979 No. 33 113 was to be found on Newton Abbot Depot.

Graham Scott-Lowe

Hydraulics

79 to 83 In the days when Diesel Hydraulic locomotives were the pride of the Western Region, Newton Abbot Depot was an excellent location for viewing Class 22s, 'Westerns', 'Hymeks', and 'Warships' in abundance. This collection of views shows these locomotives stabled, fuelling and at the washery in the early 60s.

Peter Groom
David Wood
British Rail

84 Since the withdrawal of Diesel Hydraulics from the Western Region, 'Peaks' have been more frequent visitors to the West Country. Standing beside the old and the new at Newton Abbot, the new being the diesel depot and the old being the remains of the wall from the steam depot, is No. 45 056 pictured on 1st October 1978.

David Maxey

Peaks

5 Newton Abbot is the only depot on the Western Region which possesses a traverser, an heirloom from the days when it ad its own works. This traverser occasionally used at peak mes for the stabling of locomoives. On 10th June 1978 Class 5 'Peak' No. 45 036 was seen sting there.

John Chalcraft

EXETER ST. DAVID'S S.P.

86 On the site where the old steam depot at Exeter St. David's once stood, locomotives are still to be found stabled. Although some of the original walls still remain, the depot actually lost its roof in the steam era. This view from the station shows Class 50 No. 50 001 *Dreadnought* alongside Class 31 No. 31 256 on 9th August 1977, whilst Class 33 No. 33 016 prepares to bring its train forward before working the 14.28 to Waterloo.

David Maxey

87 Stabled adjacent to the Exeter St. David's station stabling point on 20th June 1980, Class 08 shunter No. 08 479 lies at rest overlooking the station. A refurbished D.M.U. belches diesel fumes from her exhausts in the background.

Rex Kennedy

88 With a good view of the pits and recently constructed building to house diesels at Exeter St. David's stabling point, a solitary Class 33 No. 33 106 stands at the buffers. At the time of taking this photograph on 20th June 1980, the track, in fact, reached the new depot building entrance, but had yet to be laid actually inside the building.

Rex Kennedy

TAUNTON S.P.

89 A few main line diesels were often found stabled in the late 70s at Taunton stabling point. This location which frequently saw 'Warships' in their heyday is pictured here on 10th August 1976, with a Class 31 locomotive No. 31 112, a class which started its working life on the Eastern Region.

David Habgood

PLYMOUTH (Laira)

90 The new diesel depot at Laira, Plymouth was completed in 1961 and this picture shows the depot soon after completion. The general spacious layout of the yard is clearly visible, and on view are Western Region Diesel Hydraulics including one passing through the wash bay and D.M.Us bearing the green livery.

Colin Marsden Collection

92 A North British Class 22 Diesel Hydraulic locomotive No. D6329 prepares to move off the old steam depot at Laira on 27th June 1960. Glimpses of other hydraulic locomotives can be seen and in the background simmers GWR 'Grange' class locomotive No. 6823 *Oakley Grange.*
Norman Preedy

93 On 11th February 1976, Class 52 'Western' No. 1001 *Western Pathfinder* stands surrounded by the framework of a new building scheduled to become the locomotive cleaning plant at Laira.
David Habgood

94 Beneath the shear legs at Plymouth (Laira) Depot stands one of the latest residents to this West Country depot. Class 37 No. 37 142 used for china clay train workings is pictured on 30th September 1980.

M. J. Howarth

91 Overlooked by the concrete and glass structure of Laira maintenance depot on 10th August 1975, is Class 50 No. 50 011, later named *Centurion,* in front of Class 52 'Western' No. 1067 *Western Druid* with Class 25 No. 25 220 alongside.
Peter Gater

Hydraulic Parade

95 Laira Depot at Plymouth was known for an abundance of hydraulic locomotives used on both passenger and freight duties in the West Country. Two Class 42 British Railways built 'Warships', Nos. 803 *Albion* and 826 *Jupiter* stand alongside the depot building on 4th August 1969. This class was introduced in 1958 and some of the earlier locomotives in the class also worked the Exeter-Waterloo route on the Southern Region.
Barry Wynne

96 The Class 52 'Western' Diesel Hydraulic became the mainstay of power used on West Country expresses during their life between 1961, when they were first introduced, and the end of 1976 when they started being withdrawn from service. On 13th August 1975 No. 1053 *Western Patriarch*, having lost its 'D' prefix at the hands of a paint brush, rests at Laira depot.
Gavin Morrison

97 The first main line diesel locomotive to employ hydraulic transmission for running on British Railways was completed on 25th November 1957 by the North British Locomotive Company. This locomotive was numbered D600 and although, along with its class-mates, was scheduled for life on the Western Region, carried out running-in trials on the Scottish Region in the Glasgow area. One of the early members of the class No. D603 *Conquest* sits outside the depot at Laira on 7th April 1963.

Peter Groom

98 Class 42 'Warship' No. D812 *Royal Naval Reserve 1859-1959* passes through a kidney washing machine at Laira on 22nd October 1961.

British Rail

99 Cleaners apply 'V' emulsion to Class 42 'Warship' No. D867 *Zenith* at Laira Depot on 30th October 1961. This locomotive along with Nos. D866 to D870 rarely seemed to work north of Newton Abbot.

British Rail

100 Class 42 'Warship' No. D813 *Diadem* was the first to carry a four-position head-code box, and is pictured here at Laira on 7th May 1960.

John Oatway

Under Maintenance

101 Devoid of its underframe Class 47 No. 47 029 is jacked up in t maintenance depot at Laira awaiting attention on 1st October 1978.
David Max

102 The Class 50 English Electric locomotives introduced onto London Midland Region in 1967 were eventually all transferred to Western Region for use on the West Country routes, replacing the wi drawn Class 52 'Western' Diesel Hydraulics. Although the entire clas on the Western Region, major overhauls are carried out in Doncas Works, and on this occasion, 1st October 1978, having newly arri from there, No. 50 032 *Courageous* sits over the inspection pit at L Depot.

David Max

Western Lady

103 No. 1048 *Western Lady* receives a 'wash and brush up' at Laira in July 1974, before returning to duty. This locomotive, before carrying the present-day blue livery, was resplendent in maroon, and as far as the records show, never carried the green livery.

Richard Charlson

104 Lady of the Night. Illuminated by the lighting towers which give a starlight effect, No. 1048 *Western Lady* poses at Laira Depot on the evening of 10th February 1977.

Peter Walton

ST. BLAZEY

107 As Class 25 No. 25 207 stops on the turntable at St. Blazey depot on 19th June 1980, the driver climbs down to operate the mechanism which will rotate the engine.

Rex Kennedy

Turntable Scenes

108 A Class 22 North British Diesel Hydraulic locomotive No. 6330, still bearing headcodes, sits on the turntable at St. Blazey Depot on 1st May 1971. This particular locomotive generates 1,160 h.p. as did Nos. 6306 to 6357, with Nos. 6300 to 6305 generating only 1,000 h.p.

South Devon Railway Museum

105 The old half roundhouse arcing the outside turntable at St. Blazey has seen many forms of traction, from its hey-day in the steam era, the rise and fall of the hydraulic locomotives and on to giving shelter to present-day locomotives with little change to its structure. In this picture, Class 25 No. 25 048 and 'Peak' Class 46 No. 46 004 are housed at St. Blazey on 19th June 1980.

Rex Kennedy

106 Modern-day traction combines with Great Western architecture. With a fine array of entrances on view at the unique depot at St. Blazey, made to measure 'Peak' Class 46 No. 46 004 eases its way on to the turntable on 19th June 1980.

Rex Kennedy

109 Bathed in the evening sunlight streaming through the high portals of this fine old Great Western shed at St. Blazey, Class 08 shunter No. 08 377 stands over the maintenance pit on 19th June 1980. St. Blazey Depot was opened around 1872 and was originally owned by the Cornwall Minerals Railway. Each bay measured 15 ft. x 70 ft. and the three central roads were approximately 120 ft. long. Little seems to have changed since those days.

Rex Kennedy

111 Amongst the wagons and wheels at St. Blazey on 19th June 1980, Laira-based Class 25 No. 25 225 lies stabled in the yard, far from its birthplace at Darlington.

Rex Kennedy

112 The stone block building built to house the one Class 08 shunter used at Meldon Quarry stands in the shadow of the quarry workings. Inside the building is Newton Abbot allocated shunter No. 08 584 on 7th July 1979. This location is close to the famous Meldon Viaduct which used to carry the line from Exeter to Bude originally built by the London and South Western Railway.

Brian Morrison

110 Two Class 25s Nos. 25 225 and 25 080 (fitted with snow ploughs) catch the sunlight through the open portals as they rest over the pits in St. Blazey Depot on 31st March 1979. This class of locomotive was used for hauling china clay trains, the clay being prevalent in this area. This duty is now carried out by Class 37 diesels.

John Chalcraft

MELDON QUARRY

PENZANCE

113 Long Rock Depot at Penzance has now been demolished since the introduction of the new HST depot. This view of Long Rock taken in the early 1960s shows the introduction of diesel traction at Penzance. GWR 45XX tank engines along with 'Castles' etc. stand side by side with the new diesel hydraulic 'Warships'.

P. Slinn

114 On 1st August 1975, in the days when headcodes were still being used, two Brush Class 47s, Nos. 47 503 and 47 246 were pictured at Long Rock Depot, Penzance.

Brian Morrison

115 Locomotives are now stabled beside the terminus station at Penzance. The view from the road which runs beside and overlooks the station gives an interesting panorama, with buses, trains, the harbour and the buildings of Penzance beyond. On this occasion on 4th July 1980, three named locomotives are stabled. These are Nos. 50 013 *Agincourt,* with new front spotlight, 45 040 *King's Shropshire Light Infantry* and 50 047 *Swiftsure.*
Brian Morrison

116 With the building of the new HST Depot outside Penzance station, main line locomotives are stabled alongside the station. Class 50s are still a predominant feature in the West Country and on 29th September 1980 No. 50 045 *Achilles* stands at the small refuelling point.

M. J. Howarth

WORCESTER

117 Worcester, my home town for over 30 years, and the location from which I viewed the transition from steam to diesel traction, having been interested in the railway since 1943, is now merely a stabling point. Part of the old shed buildings still stand today, and this view taken in April 1975 from the station, shows three Class 31 locomotives before renumbering, standing in the spot where Great Western 'Castles' and 'Halls' once held pride of place.

Fred Kerr

118 Class 35 Beyer-Peacock 'Hymeks' were once a familiar sight at Worcester Depot. Standing in the sunshine of June 1972 No. 7016, having had its 'D' prefix obliterated, waits for its next turn of duty.

Norman Kneale

119 The shed building at Worcester pictured here on 1st July 1979, now in a rather delapidated state of repair and minus its roof, still houses a variety of motive power. A Worcester allocated Class 08 shunter No. 08 364 stands outside over the pits whilst beyond the entrance is Class 47 No. 47 422 and a solitary D.M.U.

Graham Scott-Lowe

120 Beside the shed building at Worcester are the lines which, in steam days, enthusiasts called the 'deadlines'. Class 37 No. 37 230 stands on one of these lines on 19th June 1978. These lines, now often bare, were, on Sundays, once packed with steam locomotives.

John Chalcraft

GLOUCESTER

121 This view of the maintenance shop at Gloucester gives an insight into some of the items of repair shop machinery. Class 08 shunter No. 08 804 is about to receive a new pair of leading driving wheels, which are standing over the drop pit.

Gerald Brinsford

Before Renumbering

122 During the period of time when steam and diesel could be seen together at Gloucester Depot, and when the old steam shed buildings, now gone, were still standing, this scene was a familiar sight. Class 45 'Peak' No. D89 before receiving its name *Honourable Artillery Company* stands alongside two Class 47s, Nos. D1603 and D1718 with a Great Western pannier tank in close attendance on 13th June 1965.

John Chalcraft

123 Class 45 'Peak' No. D103 with split headcode boxes and sporting the green livery, stands beside Gloucester Depot on 9th February 1969. This class of locomotive has, over the years, been a regular sight at Horton Road Depot.

Norman Preedy

124 Class 35 Diesel Hydraulic 'Hymek' No. D7052 sits in the sunshine over the pit at Horton Road Depot, Gloucester on 12th April 1968. These locomotives were built at the Beyer-Peacock works at Gorton in Manchester, the first one being delivered to British Railways in May 1961 and the final one in 1963. They were built specifically for the Western Region to replace steam power on principal passenger, parcels and freight services.

Norman Preedy

125 The buildings have gone but the pits still remain. Track maintenance equipment sits between a Class 47 locomotive and a quite unusual visitor to Gloucester Horton Road Depot, a Class 40 No. 40 109. This locomotive pictured on 7th August 1977 had spent the weekend here after arriving with a freight train. Gloucester Cathedral overlooks the scene.

Roger Kaye

126 Another unusual visitor to Gloucester Horton Road Depot is the English Electric Type 1 Class 20 locomotive. On 21st May 1978 two of these locomotives stand over the pits at Gloucester, No. 20 059 being in the foreground.

Graham Scott-Lowe

127 204 h.p. and 350 h.p. shunters stand together at Gloucester Horton Road Depot. Class 03 shunter No. 03 382 and 08 shunter No. 08 816 await repair on 1st October 1975.

Graham Wise

128 Ruston and Hornsby 0-6-0 Permanent Way Shunter No. PWM 650, allocated to Swindon, awaits maintenance at Gloucester Depot on 5th September 1978. This locomotive is one of five permanent way shunters used throughout the Western Region which were introduced onto British Railways in 1953.

Graham Scott-Lowe

BROMSGROVE S.P.

129   Class 37 English Electric Type 3 locomotives are now used for banking duties on the Lickey Incline. These locomotives are mainly called into action to assist heavy freight trains from Bromsgrove to Blackwell, after which, they return down the incline and are stabled just south of Bromsgrove station. On 23rd August 1979 Nos. 37 158 and 37 298 wait outside the mess room and administration office prior to being called for duty. The storm clouds gather over the Lickey Hills and Bromsgrove station can just be seen beyond the oil tanks. The 'Up' and 'Down' main lines are to the right of the stabled locomotives.

Gerald Brinsford

HEREFORD S.P.

130   With the ornate buildings of Hereford station providing background interest, Class 47 No. 47 166 stands alone on the stabling point used for main line locomotives on 16th August 1980.

Rex Kennedy

NEWPORT (Ebbw Junc.)

131 Newport Ebbw Junction Diesel Depot was constructed in the late 1950s. This view from the Cardiff end shows these buildings in their entirety. Usually a Cardiff allocated two-car or three-car D.M.U. set is to be found undergoing maintenance. On 14th July 1980 a Swindon cross-country set is seen with a locally allocated Class 08 shunter and a Class 37 locomotive.

Colin Marsden

132 A varied selection of motive power is pictured at Ebbw Junction on 14th October 1979. Locomotives on view include Class 37 No. 37 240, Class 25 No. 25 032, Class 40 No. 40 199 and Class 56 No. 56 033. The Class 40 locomotive is a rarity at this location but the Class 25s are used in the area on parcels trains.

Graham Scott-Lowe

134 Class 37 locomotive No. 37 284 stands beside the depot at Newport Ebbw Junction, whilst a Newport allocated 08 shunter sits in the sunlight outside the depot entrance on 20th June 1979. Details of the shunter radiator can be clearly seen.

Graham Scott-Lowe

135 A local resident at Newport Ebbw Junction is No. 47 901. This locomotive started life in October 1964 as D1628 and was allocated to Toton Depot on the London Midland Region. After being renumbered 47 046 it was involved in a collision and whilst in the workshops was converted to 47 601 and fitted with a GE 16RK3CT engine with an output of 3,250 h.p.; it was then used as a test bed for Class 56 equipment. In December 1978 this locomotive returned to Crewe Works for conversion to test bed for equipment to be fitted to the new Class 58 locomotive and received the number 47 901. Its specifications now read:-

Engine	Ruston Paxman 12RK3CT
H.P.	3,250
Tractive Effort	60,705 lbs.
Speed	80 m.p.h.
Brakes	Air only

This locomotive has frequently been seen double-headed with Class 56 locomotives on merry-go-round trains.

Graham Scott-Lowe

133 This close-up detailed portrait of the cab and front end of Class 56 No. 56 044 shows the locomotive inside Ebbw Junction Depot on 25th July 1980. The Class 56s found on Ebbw Junction are Cardiff Canton allocated and used on merry-go-round trains from either Cardiff or Newport, Didcot Power Station, Oxfordshire being their destination. These trains regularly work double-headed as far as Bristol Parkway.

Andrew Kennedy

136 Class 37 No. 37 281 stands off-duty between the main Newport to Cardiff line and Ebbw Junction shed buildings on Sunday, 5th October 1980. In the background can be seen Nos. 37 217, 37 297, 37 248 and 47 236.

Rex Kennedy

137 Standing beside the fuelling point at Newport Ebbw Junction is Class 56 No. 56 035. This locomotive has recently arrived from Toton to be used on merry-go-round train workings, and is pictured on 16th September 1979.

David Maxey

138 No. 1200 *Falcon*, once No. D0280 and bearing its crest, stands in the rear of Ebbw Junction Depot on 23rd February 1975. This locomotive spent its last days on British Rail at Newport before returning to the Brush Works at Loughborough where it was built. *Falcon* was introduced in 1961 as a prototype for the Class 47 diesel, and whilst at Newport its duties included short haul trains from Alexandra Dock Junction to Llanwern Steelworks.

Graham Scott-Lowe

139 Class 37 locomotives at Newport are used for hauling steel and coal trains to locations in the Ebbw Vale, and before the closure of Blaenavon and Hafodyrynys Collieries, in the Eastern Valleys. Locations covered include Oakdale Colliery, Bedwas Colliery, Celynen and Marine Collieries. No. 37 228 is pictured on 7th July 1974 at Ebbw Junction shed in the days when headcodes were still being used.

Rex Kennedy

140 The unusual sight of Electric Locomotives on a Western Region Depot usually means that their days are numbered. Standing at Ebbw Junction on 28th September 1978 in transit to a Newport scrapyard are Class 71 locomotives Nos. 71 002, 71 008 and 71 007.

Michael Rhodes

NEWPORT DOCKS

141 Newport Docks, once alive with steam locomotives, has now been reduced to an allocation of two Class 08 shunters. These two shunters are returned to Ebbw Junction Depot every weekend. This picture taken on 25th July 1965, during a period when one could find five or six 08 shunters in the docks, shows No. D3820 standing outside the old Newport Pill steam shed, with the transporter bridge in the background.

David Wood

ABERBEEG S.P.

142 Overlooked by the small town of Aberbeeg, Class 08 shunter No. D3821 rests in the valley on 8th November 1970. This location is no longer used for the stabling of Class 37 locomotives and there is no longer a duty for the shunter to perform.

South Devon Railway Museum

143 Aberbeeg, the junction in the Ebbw Vale for Marine Colliery and Ebbw Vale Steelworks to the north-west, and Rose Heyworth Colliery to the north, until recent years stabled a quantity of 08 shunters and Class 37 diesels at weekends. On 8th November 1970 Class 37 No. 6910 stands with a brake van in the yard.

South Devon Railway Museum

PONTYPOOL ROAD

144 Pontypool Road Depot, originally opened in 1865, once housed around 80 steam locomotives. This location is no longer used but on this occasion, in May 1967, a solitary Class 47 diesel, in green livery, stands outside the depot building.

David Thornley

SEVERN TUNNEL JUNCTION

145 Severn Tunnel Junction is the one location on the Western Region that sees practically every class of diesel locomotive. The depot is, in fact, a distribution point and trains from all regions arrive, are split up and re-formed, and taken on into Wales hauled by Cardiff Canton allocated locomotives. In the same way, the locomotives that arrive from all over Britain return to their respective regions in charge of other trains. A variety of traction is seen in this picture on 16th September 1979, including two Class 20s Nos. 20 185 and 20 171. Class 20s always arrive at Severn Tunnel in multiple and return in the same form, and are usually from the Toton area.

Brian Morrison

146 Many freight trains arrive at Severn Tunnel Junction in the early hours of the morning. One in particular is from Moss End on the Scottish Region and is often hauled by a Class 40 locomotive. Class 40s also arrive from the Warrington area, but on every occasion they approach the junction from Hereford and not through the tunnel. On 3rd October 1979 No. 40 025 stands outside the office building.

Graham Scott-Lowe

148 Class 52 'Western' No. D1012 *Western Firebrand* from Plymouth (Laira) and sporting the maroon livery, stands in line outside the fuelling depot at Severn Tunnel Junction with Class 47 No. D1727 (now 47 135) and Class 37 No. D6879 (now 37 179) on 26th August 1966.

Barry Wynne

147 A line of main-line locomotives lie stabled on the morning of Saturday, 9th August 1980 at Severn Tunnel Junction. The line up comprises No. 37 183 from Landore, at the head of Nos. 47 109, 37 292, 47 099, 47 244, 45 036, 47 097 and 47 347. These locomotives have arrived on a variety of freight trains, from coal and chemicals to steel and motor cars. One of the six shunters from Ebbw Junction, allocated for duty at Severn Tunnel, is designated to haul the car trains on arrival to the old steam depot, which is now a car distribution centre. These trains, more often than not, bring Ford motor cars from Garstang and Dagenham, but a few trains also arrive from the continental ports with Chrysler and Opel cars.

Rex Kennedy

149 A rather uncommon sight at Severn Tunnel Junction is that of a Class 50 locomotive. No. 50 049 *Defiance* lies stabled beside the fuelling bay on 20th June 1979. The variety of traction to be found at Severn Tunnel substantiates the fact that the crews employed at this depot are trained to drive, with the exception of Class 56 locomotives, all main line diesels.

Graham Scott-Lowe

150 Locomotives are stabled beneath the road bridge at Severn Tunnel Junction after having been refuelled at the fuelling point. On this occasion on 9th August 1980, Class 45 'Peak' No. 45 074 is awaiting its return to duty. The fuelling point at Severn Tunnel was built in the mid 1960s and replaced the old steam depot at the other end of the station. It is interesting to note that all non air-braked freight stock from the London area heading for the West Country, must first call at Severn Tunnel Junction for checking, before continuing its journey.

Rex Kennedy

Freight Locomotives

152 The footbridge entrance into Cardiff (Canton) Depot which passes over the main line, is familiar to all railway enthusiasts from the days of steam to the present day. Beside the bridge, on 14th July 1974, stands Class 37 No. 37 284 together with the Canton based snowplough.

Barry Nicolle

153 Before the introduction of the Class 56 locomotives to Cardiff (Canton) Class 20s were allocated to this depot for a short period. No. 20 179 stands at the buffers near the depot entrance on 14th May 1979.

Graham Scott-Lowe

154 Seen through the entrance of the fuelling depot at Cardiff (Canton) on 16th September 1979, is the newly arrived Class 56 No. 56 040, allocated to Canton for merry-go-round workings.

David Maxey

151 Standing beneath the hoist used for lifting locomotive bodies for bogie changing is Derby Works Class 116/1 diesel unit No. W51148 at Cardiff (Canton) on 5th October 1980. Owing to a fold in the front indicator blind, the destination shown appears to be Barry Isand.

Rex Kennedy

155 The 650 h.p. Paxman Diesel Hydraulics were introduced in 1964 on to the Western Region for short distance freight duties. In Wales this generally entailed coal haulage. On 3rd April 1965 No. D9529 lies stabled on the depot at Cardiff (Canton).

John Scrace

156 Outside the maintenance depot at Cardiff (Canton) is the locally based Class 08 shunter No. 08 195 on 17th September 1978.

Graham Scott-Lowe

157 The 09 shunters are rarely seen anywhere except on the Southern Region. The sight, therefore, of No. 09 024 at Cardiff (Canton) Depot on 9th November 1979 is very unusual.

Graham Scott-Lowe

158 Class 45 'Peak' No. 45 052 seen at Canton on 21st October 1975, not only displays its T.O.P.S. number but also its old number, 75. A good view of the structure of the maintenance depot adds interest to the picture.

Graham Scott-Lowe

159 This view of the fuelling depot at Cardiff (Canton) illustrates well its design. At the station end stand Nos. 31 421, 47 196, 47 518 and 56 040 on 5th October 1980.

Rex Kennedy

160 An invader from the Southern Region to Cardiff (Canton) is Class 33 No. 33 025 having arrived on 13th May 1978 with a 'special'.

Michael Rhode.

161 Undergoing servicing at Cardiff (Canton) Depot is Class 37 No. 6921 (now 37 221). This class of locomotive is used extensively for heavy coal trains to and from the valleys, and this particular locomotive, pictured in August 1973, was later allocated to the Eastern Region at Immingham Depot.

Barry Wynne

Under Maintenance

162 The large maintenance depot at Cardiff (Canton) has facilities for dealing with many locomotives at the same time. In August 1973, Class 37 No. 6993 undergoes maintenance in the same bay as Beyer-Peacock 'Hymek' No. D7080.

Barry Wynne

163 Emitting steam and bearing the locomotive number 1013 in the headcode panel, Class 52 'Western' *Western Ranger* rests over the inspection pit in the maintenance depot at Cardiff (Canton) on 4th February 1977.

Peter Walton

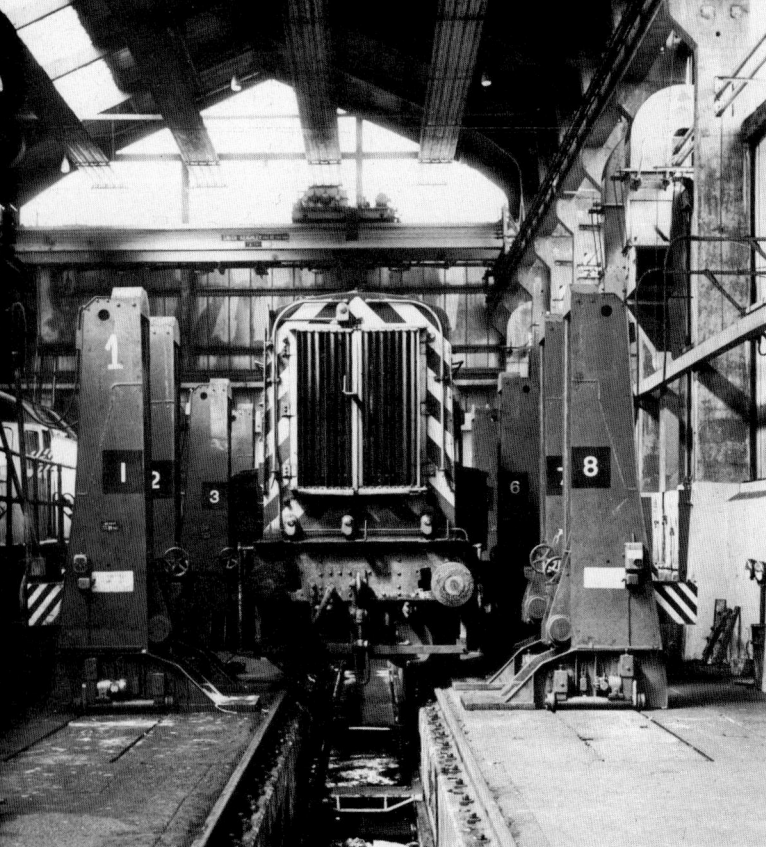

164 The Ruston and Hornsby 0-6-0 P.W.M. locomotives have now received T.O.P.S. numbering. No. 97651, once PWM 651, which is usually to be found in Radyr Yard, receives maintenance at Cardiff (Canton) along with Nos. 25 042 and 47 256 on 5th October 1980.

Rex Kennedy

166 Main line diesels are often to be found coupled to the head of a passenger train within the confines of the carriage shed at Cardiff (Canton). On 9th November 1979 Class 45 'Peak' No. 45 003 waits to return to duty with its train.

Graham Scott-Lowe

167 Since the introduction of HSTs into Wales, the sight of these trains in the carriage shed at Cardiff (Canton) is a familiar one. Here, on 5th October 1980, we see set No. 253 010, the leading car being W43020.

Rex Kennedy

165 A locally based Class 08 shunter nestles within the area of the mechanical body hoists at Cardiff (Canton) Depot.

Michael Rhodes

253 010

168 Winter conditions prevailed on Monday, 20th February 1978, providing an added dimension to the picture. Amongst a varied collection of locomotives is Class 31 No. 31 118 and Class 40 No. 40 177 with windscreen completely obscured.
Michael Rhodes

169 Bearing a light frosting of snow on its roof Class 40 No. 40 177, having failed after working Crewe to Cardiff train two days earlier, lies dorma on Cardiff (Canton) Depot on 20th February 1978.
Michael Rhod

170 After a sub-zero weekend in Wales, Class 2 No. 25 058 along with Class 47 No. 47 033 show e dence of the wintry conditions at Cardiff (Canto on 20th February 1978.

Michael Rhod

171 Class 37 No. 37 188 returns to the fuelling bay at Cardiff (Canton) on 16th April 1978, after working the Gwili R.P.S. Railtour to Brighton the previous day.

David Maxey

172 The interesting roof design of the fuelling depot at Cardiff (Canton) is well illustrated in this picture. Class 45 'Peak' No. 45 023 *The Royal Pioneer Corps* is stabled beside the depot on 5th October 1980.

Rex Kennedy

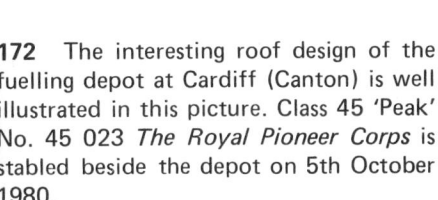

173 Derby three-car units used for services into the valleys from Cardiff undergo maintenance in the D.M.U. depot at Cardiff (Canton) on 16th April 1978. Both units on view bear the new refurbished livery.

David Maxey

D.M.Us.

174 In comparison, Diesel Multiple Unit bearing the old green livery and having a distinctive front panel are seen at Cardiff (Canton) in the maintenance depot on 27th January 1959.

British Ra...

175 Departmental single car diesel unit No. ADB 975659 (ex W55035) poses outside the D.M.U. depot at Cardiff (Canton) on 5th October 1980.

Rex Kennedy

176 Beside the D.M.U. maintenance depot at Cardiff (Canton) are the fuelling points and yards for the stabling of the Cardiff units. On 5th October 1980, refurbished Derby Works Class 116/1 three-car suburban set headed by No. W51152 lies stabled with Class 120/1 Swindon Works three-car cross-country set, the leading car being No. W51579. The difference in liveries should be noted.

Rex Kennedy

CARDIFF DOCKS S.Ps.

177 Cardiff Docks, once the location of the well-known Cardiff East Dock steam depot housing many locomotives, is now only serviced by two Class 08 diesel shunters. Whilst off duty, one of these shunters is stabled at Queen Alexandra Dock and on 5th October 1980 No. 08 351 was seen amidst the dockland environment at this location.
Rex Kennedy

178 Dwarfed by cranes at Roath Dock, Class 08 shunter No. 08 193 lies stabled on Sunday, 5th October 1980. It should be noted that this particular locomotive still carries the wooden door to the cab. Diesel shunters used on Cardiff Docks are all serviced at Canton Depot. The clearcall mechanism is fitted to this shunter. This device is used on dock shunters for contact with the control points in the docks.

Rex Kennedy

RADYR

179 The old steam depot at Radyr opened in 1931 and situated at the Cardiff end of the yard, is no longer used for the stabling of diesel locomotives. This view taken on 20th July 1965 shows a predominance of Class 37 locomotives which operated from Radyr for use on heavy freight trains in the Cardiff valleys.

David Wood

180 During the period when steam locomotives were being stored at the end of the yard at Radyr, diesels were used for moving these around. On 25th July 1965, 0-6-0 Paxman No. D9534 performs this duty. In the background is the old depot turntable.

David Wood

181 Class 08 shunters and Class 37s are now stabled in the yard at Radyr, and a common sight with these Cardiff allocated Class 37s is the painting of the T.O.P.S. number on the front of the locomotive. On 16th April 1978 two of these locomotives are seen stabled together with No. 37 280 in the foreground. At one time, locomotives were also stabled beside the station, but owing to the close proximity of housing this location ceased to be used.

David Maxey

182 Locomotives are stabled outside the old steam depot at Barry in which wagons are now kept. This depot was opened as long ago as 1893 and the type of traction seen there today is predominantly Class 37 and 47 locomotives. On this occasion, 15th September 1979, locomotives stabled included Nos. 37 257, 37 270, 37 280 and 37 255.

Brian Morrison

183 On 9th July 1979 a solitary Class 47 locomotive stood outside the old steam depot at Barry. This locomotive was No. 47 186; a far-off cry from the days in 1948 when one could see up to 80 steam locomotives on shed.

Gerald Brinsford

LLANTRISANT

184 In 1964 one could see both steam and diesel traction at the old steam shed at Llantrisant. Standing outside the shed building, which opened in 1900, is English Electric Type 3, Class 37 No. D6841 on 4th September 1964.

Peter Groom

185 Today, locomotives at Llantrisant are stabled alongside the main line, near to the old goods shed. On 9th July 1979 Class 08 shunter No. 08 187 waits at the stabling point, whilst Class 37 No. 37 239 brings an empty coal train into Llantrisant yard.

Gerald Brinsford

RHYMNEY S.P.

DOWLAIS (Cae Harris)

188 Nothing now remains of the old steam depot at Dowlais Cae Harris which was built in 1876, but on 24th July 1975, a solitary Class 37 No. D6974 was to be found at this location. A freight only line still exists up the steep incline to within a mile of Dowlais Cae Harris.

David Wood

186 Rhymney is one of the valley termini for D.M.U. services to and from Cardiff. Units are stabled, on occasions, in one of the disused platforms at Rhymney station and on 16th September 1979 a refurbished Derby three-car set is seen at this location.

David Maxey

TREHERBERT

189 Use of old steam depots in the South Wales valleys was commonplace around 1965, but Treherbert was soon to be discontinued as a stabling point. This view of Class 37 locomotives and a diesel hydraulic Paxman taken on 24th July 1975 shows the depot building as it was, when built, in 1931.

David Wood

ABERCYNON

190 Abercynon, situated at the junction of the Merthyr line and Aberdare line, now has no stabling facilities for diesel locomotives. On 24th July 1965, English Electric Type 3, Class 37 No. D6832 stands motionless outside the old steam depot.

David Wood

187 The line at Rhymney continues for a short distance to a point north of the station, and this is used also for the stabling of multiple units. Two refurbished Cardiff based three-car sets were at this location on 16th September 1979.

David Maxey

ABERDARE

191 Aberdare once boasted a fine round house building. The depot was opened i. 1907 and closed in 1965, being used for th stabling of diesel locomotives in its latte years. A Paxman Diesel Hydraulic locomo tive No. D9540 showing a fine example c the BR crest stands off duty inside th depot on 24th July 1965.

David Woo

193 The diesel depot at Margam serves the large marshalling yards nearby which were officially opened on 11th April 1960. ▶ When opened, it was one of the largest and most modern hump yards in the country, and probably, the first completely automatic yard in Europe. The yard itself occupies some 180 acres and contains approximately 33 miles of rail. The west end of the depot with Nos. 37 277, 37 287, 47 241 and 08 366 is pictured here on 5th October 1980.

Rex Kennedy

192 Locomotives at Aberdare are now stabled behind the old high level station. A Class 08 shunter and a small quantity of Class 37 diesels can be found, generally at this situation. This view, taken on 13th May 1979, gives a typical weekend picture at Aberdare.

Rex Kennedy

194 Class 56 locomotives at Margam operate in pairs with steel trains from Port Talbot to Llanwern Steelworks. These replaced triple-headed Class 37 locomotives and trains run full to Llanwern and empty back to Port Talbot. The load now consists of 35 x 100 ton wagons with a gross weight of 3,800 tons, the heaviest train in Britain today. Wagons have rotary couplings, and therefore are never uncoupled but stay together on a permanent basis. No. 56 043 stands off duty over the pits at Margam beside Class 08 shunter No. 08 367 on 16th September 1979.

David Maxey

195 Class 37 No. 37 291 rests for the day in Margam depot on 5th October 1980 prior to receiving minor maintenance.

Rex Kennedy

196 The unusual design of the 0-6-0 Diesel Hydraulic Paxman locomotive is clearly visible in this view taken on 24th July 1965 outside Margam depot. This class of locomotive, No. D9543 pictured here, never reached the stage of T.O.P.S. numbering.

David Wood

197 In the hey-day of the Class 52 'Western' locomotive, these engines could often be found standing at Margam Depot. On 7th July 1974, No. 1049 *Western Monarch* nestles between a Class 45 'Peak' and a Class 47 locomotive.

Rex Kennedy

198 Beside the maintenance building at Margam, with the Port Talbot Steelworks in the distance, stands a Class 56 locomotive, No. 56 033 together with Class 37 No. 37 304 on 13th September 1979.

Brian Morrison

199 The design of the depot building at Margam is clearly shown in this picture. A Margam allocated Class 08 shunter No. 08 362 stands with a Class 46 'Peak' No. 46 057 on 13th September 1979. Other locomotives on view are Nos. 47 512, 37 304 and 37 188. Class 46 locomotives are not an uncommon sight at Margam.

Brian Morrison

200 Beyond the end of the depot yard at Margam is the Margam Sorting Sidings Signal Box. Beyond this point in the direction of the Port Talbot Steelworks, Class 37 locomotives are regularly stabled. On 5th October 1980 six of these locomotives stood in line. No. 37 192 bearing the front head lamps stands at the head of Nos. 37 302, 37 247, 37 307, 37 301 and 37 270.

Rex Kennedy

201 The diesel depot at Landore, Swansea was built in 1963 for the purpose of servicing and maintaining Type 3 and Type 4 Diesel Electric locomotives, and Type 1 and Type 3 Diesel Hydraulic units. The depot was built on the site of the old steam depot, in a triangle, bounded by the London to Swansea main line and the Swansea to Fishguard line. Major maintenance is carried out here in the three servicing roads. This particular view shows the depot structure with three Class 47 locomotives Nos. 47 089 *Amazon*, 47 064 and 47 075 on 24th May 1980 with Class 08 shunter No. 08 354 in close attendance.

John Augustson

202 Locomotives are also stabled on lines beside the depot buildings, and on 5th October 1980 Class 37 No. 37 177 stands on one of these lines, and in the distance is seen Class 08 shunter No. 08 663.

Rex Kennedy

203 English Electric Type 3 locomotives receive attention in the heavy maintenance area at Landore on 4th July 1973.

Colin Marsden

204 An unusual sight in any depot is that of a locomotive bearing no number. Here undergoing maintenance at Landore on 5th October 1980 is Class 37 No 37 273 with a glimpse of Class 03 shunter No. 03 144 in the adjacent bay.

Rex Kennedy

205 One of the features of a visit to Landore Diesel Depot is the chance to see the Class 03 shunters with the cut down cabs. Here we see Nos. 03 119 and 03 120 together in the fuelling depot on 16th April 1978.

David Maxey

206 A fine study of the features of a Class 47 locomotive outside the depot at Landore on 5th October 1980. No. 47 282 rests before returning to duty together with Class 08 shunter No. 08 664.

Rex Kennedy

SWANSEA EAST DOCK S.P.

207 Beside the main road from Swansea to Cardiff on the outskirts of Swansea the track runs parallel with the road for a short while, through the dockland. Near to the point where Swansea East Dock steam depot once stood, Class 37 locomotives are stabled at weekends along with brake-vans and Class 08 shunters. In this view pictured on 16th September 1979, are Nos. 37 251, 37 296, 37 238 and 37 217.

David Maxey

NEATH (N&B)

208 Neath (N&B) Depot was the onl
depot on the old Neath and Brecon Railwa
and was situated near Neath Riversid
station. The building seen in this picture i
of the depot as rebuilt in 1946/47. This loca
tion, alas, is no more, but on 24th July 196
Class 08 shunter No. D3403 stood outsid
with an unidentified Class 37 in the buildin
David Woo

LLANELLI S.P.

209 Locomotives at Llanelli are stabled both inside and out, and on 30th August 1980, three Class 37s occupied the undercover accommodation. The three on view are Nos. 37 284, 37 287 and 37 190.

A. French

210 Stabled in the open at Llanelli on 24th May 1980 are four Class 03 shunters with cut down cabs and front headlight. This type of locomotive is used for shunting duties extensively in this part of Wales, and on this occasion Nos. 03 151, 03 120, 03 141 and 03 119 are pictured.

John Augustson

BURRY PORT S.P.

211 Burry Port stabling point near Pembury is the location on the main line where the Class 03 shunters, used for working to Cwmmawr on the Burry Port and Gwendraeth Valley line, are to be found. Stabled in the siding, on 12th September 1979, are Nos. 03 119, 03 145, 03 141 and 03 152, all with cut down cabs and headlights for working this remote line.

Brian Morrison

CARMARTHEN

212 After a long spell of non-existence of any form of depot building at Carmarthen, a new brick and corrugated iron structure was built in 1979. This building is large enough to take one main line diesel, and on 11th September 1979, Class 47 No. 47 104 stands beside it.

Brian Morrison

213 Pantyffynnon on the Central Wales line, which runs between Llanelli and Shrewsbury, is the one location used for the stabling of freight locomotives which operate in this area. The one feature of the Class 37 locomotives to be found here is the inclusion of the front headlight used on the Central Wales line. Pictured here on 24th May 1980 are Nos. 37 185, 37 177 together with two Class 08 shunters Nos. 08 577 and 08 819.

John Augustson

PANTYFFYNNON